THE HISTORIES

THE HISTORIES

Jason Whitmarsh

Carnegie Mellon University Press
Pittsburgh 2017

ACKNOWLEDGMENTS

Some of these poems first appeared in *The Cincinnati Review, The Monarch Review, Ploughshares, Poetry Northwest, Puerto del Sol, Subtropics,* and *Alive at the Center* (Ooligan Press). My thanks to the editors.

Thanks to the Helen Riaboff Whiteley Center for providing the time and space to write some of these poems.

Thanks to my friends who write with me: Rebecca Hoogs, Sierra Nelson, Rachel Kessler, Kevin Craft, Richard Kenney, Julie Larios, Catherine Wing, and Adina Hagege.

Cody Walker has read these poems dozens of times (and a thousand other poems of mine only once). Thanks for that judgment, and for your inspiration and friendship.

Thanks to my family: my children, my father and stepmother, my mother and stepfather, my brothers and sisters: Megan, Ian, Holden, Colin, and always Amy.

Thanks most of all to Kerry.

Book design by Danielle Lehmann

Library of Congress Control Number 2016948992
ISBN 978-0-88748-622-7
Copyright © 2017 by Jason Whitmarsh
Printed and bound in the United States of America

10 9 8 7 6 5 4 3 2 1

CONTENTS

for Margaret, Henry, and Oliver

HISTORY OF THE HORSEMEN

A horseman was found horseless on the side of the road. We asked after his horse, but he had no recollection, of a horse or of his having been a horseman. And so how were we so sure? How did we know this was a man who lacked the very thing that defined him? We knew because we ourselves were horsemen, and we ourselves without horses.

HISTORY OF THE HEART

The heart was at first external to the body, and held in the hand, and manipulated by punch cards. Experts trailed the heart as it went into alleys, across yards, through the ravines of crushed velvet. Questions were yes/no and took years to answer. The heart was PVC tubing and quarter-minus and known to be involuntary. The heart was rechargeable in only the most technical sense. Left in the sun, the heart demanded the moon. Left in the moon, the heart demanded the wind. Later, the heart was in the chest, the head, the tips of the fingers. By means of various surgical techniques and dark rooms, by means of water and spooled wire, by means of a sudden and upward motion, the heart that was yours was not yours and then was yours again.

INTO TWO

The time machine, if invented, will mainly affect the next edition of *The Chicago Manual of Style*. The future perfect will have to extend to what will now have already happened in the past. "I will averted the assassination," *The Chicago Manual of Style* will say that you can say. "I will saw you" will no longer be reserved for magicians and their unhappy assistants.

HISTORY OF NOSTALGIA

Two hundred years ago, the Swiss mercenaries miss their Saturday morning cartoons. They grow drowsy, emaciated, cold to the touch. Surgeons are brought in, television licensing deals arranged, small windows propped open for the invigorating air. *Speed Racer*, for example: No one remembers the 4-frames-per-second choppiness (the Swiss mercenaries will tell you, weeping). To recount what we have lost is to lose it again. To listen to the *Kuhreihen* is to know you will always listen to it, as Odysseus continues to hear the Sirens, a low flood of exacting joy beneath all that anyone is saying.

HISTORY OF MODEL TRAIN ENCAMPMENTS

1.

In the first model train villages, the tiny houses are occupied by mermaids, women with aprons and bonnets and silver tails tucked beneath rocking chairs. Mermaid babies cry from their cribs.

2.

R. builds model train village farmhouses and takes pictures of them and shows them to people who can or cannot tell the difference between the model's photo and the real thing's photo. This is a long time after the mermaids have left. In the model train villages these days, no one makes a sound.

3.

You get up in the morning and excuse yourself and head outside, where the model trains run. The tracks are listing northward, a problem with the plywood base. The gravel is sand, and the trees twigs, and so on, right down to your painted-on shoes. Hildred writes and says to come to the country.

4.

Oh ho and all that. The armies culled from the model train village bars and factories are not yet up to snuff. They'd be overrun in any serious campaign. We must arm them with model train Manhattan Projects. We must invest in their science programs, in their blackboards and slide rules. Hildred telegraphs that it's no use, the country is no more and she's found someone else. Even the tunnels never reach pitch black before bursting again into the light.

HISTORY OF THERAPY

The king has dismantled the castle and taken up meditation and convinced his knights to lay down their swords, to strip off their chain mail, to lift up not only their visors but the entire helmet, it's a weight you never needed, the king says, imploringly, between chants. The sun unhooks from the trees and rises into a deep and unrecognizable sky. Several birds say something to several other birds. It's only later that the king sees what those helmets were for, how excellent that chain mail was at preventing impalement, how a castle has evolved over a thousand years to dull the attention of the returning dragon.

HISTORY OF PARANOIA

The self-administered questionnaire meant to identify Martians produces frequent false positives: the English; rural Canadians; anyone raised without a television. Talking horses. False negatives could be happening just as frequently, it's hard to know. There's no other way of identifying the Martians, it's only this take-home exam with the stamped pre-addressed envelope. Most everyone could be a false negative, and eyeing us, and reading our minds, and nightly detentacling. As with other tests designed by this service, and fairy tales, and much of adult life in general, there have been no true positives.

HISTORY OF ROBOTICS

Robots were first of cardboard and only later of metal, or plastic, or flesh. The cardboard robots played chess in Washington Square and dried the dishes in post-World-War-II Japan. Hopelessness was a big problem for them, as well as shame at having got a thing wrong, such as falling for the Queen's Gambit, or drying not a cup but the bald head of an old man. We solve shame by trying to do what's right the next time around, and hopelessness by looking outside in the spring and saying, you see? You see? Even the cardboard robots know this is a case of one thing standing in for another: a hummingbird replacing the flower's flower, a timetable outperforming the water marks on the trees.

HISTORY OF TRAVEL

Those who have made the journey have never returned. They plummeted from the edge (one theory), or disappeared in the storm, or died of thirst between wells. Actually, some have returned, but it was a long time later, when they no longer spoke our language, and their eyes were sunken, and we'd forgotten their names. Well, in truth several have returned after only a few days, with suntans and stacks of photos. But the photos were blurry, or too saturated, or not of us.

HISTORY OF TITLES

The first title was just the story itself, but in a bigger font. The second title was the first title, followed by a two. Title three was untitled, but written out: "Untitled." And so on, for a couple thousand years. Nowadays, the raw materials for titles come mostly from Eastern Europe, and are stitched together by bored children in their short-equipment playgrounds. Children need to be more than two feet off the ground to feel joy, just as titles must come together from an untutored process of apparition and staple gun. The sweet spot for titles is the painting, because the title doesn't even appear on the painting itself. Some galleries have placed titles on the opposite coast from the paintings they represent. Titles are the pneumatic tubes of our ideas, quick and, despite all further technical advances, satisfying in their complete and sudden delivery of information. Some titles have been used to solve famous murder cases, others to diagnose terrible diseases, diseases that ravaged much of Britain before we met. In the near future, titles will give way to footnotes. And footnotes to just the number signifying the footnote, and the number to just the height of the number, the height and the size. You must picture a version of yourself 30% smaller and suspended in the air halfway above your head.

HISTORY OF TRANSLATION

The joke "How many surrealists does it take to change a light bulb?" becomes, in German, "How many surrealists—the answer, by the way, is fish—does it take to change a light bulb? Fish, yes, that's correct. *Sehr gut.*"

HISTORY OF THE PROSE POET

He gathers all she's done into a single paragraph. The snapped skateboard, the six months in France, the insomnia, the children, the all of it. Read it with the right intonation, he says, and you really come to life. Pages 7 to 28 are out of order, she says. I was in Scotland before Morocco, and Morocco before West Lafayette. And the dozens of starlings were only two or three at most. You never have me blinking, or leaving early, or catching my skirt in the car door. I've done those things, don't you think? And others, too. "Overjoyed" should be italicized.

HISTORY OF MONEY: THE EARLY YEARS

Right after language came money, which was too bad. We were hoping for love, first, or a good joke. We were angling for cooperative living arrangements and card games. We were thinking it could've been fantasies during sex, or cool nicknames, or singing. Instead, someone said can I have a bite of that, I can owe you, and we said well how do we know? How will we remember, with all this hunting and gathering, that you're in the red with us, berry-wise?

HISTORY OF THE HYPOTHETICAL

We were exactly as we had been, but unable to read novels set in a different season from the one we were experiencing. Some of us had it so bad we could read only the parts of books set on the same day of the year, and some of us were less bad, and just needed a description of snow when it got cold out. The worst cases watched Christmas movies only on Christmas, and only those Christmas movies that took place in real time, that lasted the two hours that you spent watching. Any stretching of real time, any ten minutes of movie time that took place over two actual minutes, say, induced a kind of vertigo. If a movie showed a year passing too quickly, the worst cases fell into a trance, all of them dreaming the hands-of-a-clock dream, in which the second hand is ever so slightly off from an actual second, and then catches up, and then is off, and then catches up, and then is off.

HISTORY OF THE SODA MACHINE

The soda machine is touchscreen and allows extensive flavor combinations, such as Vanilla Peach Strawberry Coke. When they say our lives are getting too complicated, they usually mean this soda machine, whose choices exceed any meaningful rules we've made about adjectives and wish fulfillment. The soda machine is unable, at present, to experience love, or express itself only with its eyes, or render known what is unknowable, or deliver what I'd call a normal amount of ice.

HISTORY OF THE CREATION MYTH

—I got the candy, the kind with the small rocks in the center.

—The ones with the breastbone?

—No, that's not candy, the ones with the breastbone. That's people.

—Oh. The ones with the eyes and the always saying, "Hmm, I don't think so"?

—Still people.

—The ones with the long books and the constant stories of how things are pretty bad now and getting worse but were so much better twenty years ago?

—Yeah, OK, those. But with rocks in the middle.

—I had those too. They were not as advertised. First of all—

—I think we're talking about two different things.

—First of all, no mention of a philosophy that I, myself, can apply to anything.

—Mm, I don't know about that. There was the being—

—Second of all, no historical record of me.

—Yeah, that happens. They forget, maybe.

—Forget forgetting—it's like me never happened, as far as they care.

—Well you got company. I never happened either.

—Yeah, there's that. The two of us, never happening—can you think it?

—I just keep thinking rock, rocks, rocks.

—Probably for the best.

HISTORY OF LOSS

I keep having to count my brothers and sisters, now: M. and I. are one and two, C. and H. are three and four. And who is five? Oh, she was five. And who is six? Oh, I am six.

BARELY TRANSLATED ITALIAN LETTER

In the letter from
1937, she
writes about 19-

38. So, a
year ahead. She says "therefore"
twice in one line. So,

unhappy. No one
says therefore that much if
they're feeling joyful,

which she says just once.
"Joyful" is a long way from
"always," which she says

later, and about
something else. Also, "careful,"
"my," "itself," "these." In

the Basilica
of St. Clement, the eagle
is no eagle and

the snake is no snake.
Still, best is to be careful,
like Romulus,

with his ring of stone.
When he said "you'll be safe," he
meant only for now.

SCALE

On a scale of dog
tag to metallic clang, it
was whistle. On a

scale of osmium
to iridium, it was
Uuo, placeholder

for element one
eighteen, provisionally
discovered by the

Russians. On a scale
of this sunset to sunrise,
it was yet to be

independently
verified. Humans are the
only animal

to use tools to make
machines they later have
to apologize

for. On a scale of
that woman saying "sorry"
to a man on the

ground, it was horse. Next
to Uuo is Uuh, ele-
ment one sixteen and

also Russian and
also unpictured and al-
so provisional.

NIGHT SONG

Every Jill is leaving
and every Jack's awake.
That's him, keening;
that's her, at the gate.
The birds are afterwards
and the rain's just before.
The trees all mean well;
the coffin's an open door.

HISTORY OF CORRESPONDENCE

The people you write only the shortest of notes to, get well, I'm thinking of you. The people you write your life story to. The people you misrepresent yourself to, the people you don't know how to sign off to, the people you never write to in the first place. The people you write to who don't write back, the people you don't write to who write to you. The people you write to only by forwarding what you've already written. The people you write to not by forwarding but by copying and pasting a paragraph you wrote to some other, better-loved people. The people you mail letters to, send emails to, text, call, call when you know they're not likely to answer. The voice messages you leave those people. The outgoing messages those people set up in the first place, the messages that sound like they're answering the phone, the messages that sound like they're nervous, the messages that sound like they're on their fifth attempt, the messages that in no way anticipate what you will tell them.

DEAR M.

You won't believe what arrived in the—a hedgehog! Yes, yes, of course, and steel netting, and gloves that work. "Hans My," we think, and behind the stove for the first nine years. We'll have to keep an eye on that rooster, and those kings, and bagpipes. Truth is, I'll be glad (the heart breaks to ever say it) when he's dead. May we outlive all such children.

HISTORY OF MACGYVER

MacGyver, aged 17, escapes a locked car using a toothpick and a can of aerosol. MacGyver, aged 8, plunges twelve stories into a dump truck. He emerges unscathed, carrying a nearly translucent umbrella. MacGyver, aged 14 months, establishes contact with a friendly behind enemy lines using a pacifier, an English muffin, and a Glock. MacGyver, in utero, counts his possessions: 10 soft fingernails, a fine, potentially braidable hair covering everything, any number of already vestigial parts: the muscles of the ear, gills, the tailbone, the tiny appendix.

HISTORY OF THE LOVE SONG

She ran a bar called the Robot's Right Arm and he proofread *Wheel of Fortune* entries for curse words. She thought two hawks and a fern tree meant long life, not mysterious stranger, and he couldn't find the translation for "songbird" in the Icelandic-English dictionary. The stranger stood in the eelgrass with his one eye and low-brimmed hat. She had to repeat his name to keep from forgetting it: Odin, Odin, Odin. Imagine the word "FULLBACK," he explains, and the contestant says F, C, K, and I'd like to buy a U. The *Wheel of Fortune* in Iceland is a terrible show, she says. Everyone guesses the Viking letters first. He was raised by wolves in a forest and she likes the center of a room, the way it situates her sadness. The king grows pale and wanders far from his castle. The queen looks in on no sleeping children. The sleeping children call out for their missing gods.

HISTORY OF LOVE

Most poems since 1776 include the lines "it was snowing and it was going to snow," although only Wallace Stevens in 1917 got it exactly right. Since 1776, I have caused you heartache, I know, except for 1995, when we were in Chicago and happy in a way that was both fragile and fast-paced, like we were outrunning some terrible collapse. Wallace Stevens was dead and all around us, mostly in the nonsense of the car alarms, the snowplow on Lake Shore Drive, the lake itself with its waves frozen into place. Ice means: this is no permeable surface. You will not sink and drown, but neither will you be enclosed.

HISTORY OF THE NON-QUIET DEVO

Of the thousands of Devos, it was not so difficult to pick the ones who would make music.

*

There were at this time the castle-dwelling Devos, the confrontational Devos, the hundreds of philosophical Devos, and (up the stairs and to your right) the non-quiet Devos.

*

Terrible news was when some not-insignificant portion of Devos (the Cornish-hen Devos, the table-setting Devos, the world-weary Devos) would at once disappear, Atlantis-like. Also terrible was when you listened to the non-quiet Devos in your bedroom in eighth grade and your Dad said this was absurd, you'd never keep listening to them, and then, three years later, you never did keep listening to them.

*

The Devos arrived before the cell phone, the single-sourced American chocolate bar, and the time-traveler Kevlar suit, but, nevertheless, they were from and of the future. Unstable combinations of Devos that were quick to disappear included cowboy Devos and hand-mopping Devos.

*

Some nights, at 3 a.m., try waking up suddenly, as if throwing a switch. The moon flooding the room, the small hum of the streetlight, the exhaustion of the day ahead, and the day ahead of that. There, in the corner—is it Ghost Devo? Is it Child Devo? Is it Limitless Devo? We shall mourn them all.

HISTORY OF FEAR

In our agreement to not be stone, to instead have a season, to notice that the clouds can resemble things that are not clouds, to name our children, to wake up at 2 a.m. and want to talk, to talk, in our agreement to have these things, to notice the exact angle of light, to watch the way a tree in the wind seems to shake with laughter, in our holding up of hands to measure the sun, in this agreement of recognition and revision, we agreed, too, to take on fear. The gods wanted us to have something they didn't, is how they put it, and we still at that point thought everything was worth wanting.

HISTORY OF BOARD GAMES

No one ever invented Hasbro Poetry Death Match, not once. Hence the need for radio, television, pinball, and sex. Hence turnstile jumpers and Tuesday-afternoon bong hits. Hence fencing scholarships. In Hasbro Poetry Death Match, all the players are usually dead by round two. Round *two*. Compare that to your typical grocery store visit. In the rare event a winner is declared, the party starts up immediately and only stops when another Shakespeare walks in.

HISTORY OF ADVERTISING

The world's last advertisement was a billboard in Las Vegas that described the Moorea topless resort as "toptional." What there was after that was a lot of blank spaces in our cities, on our televisions, in our magazines, on our computer screens. Entire songs disappeared, entire characters in entire movies went dark. The advertisements in our conversations were now just silence: no one could tell you why they got that watch, why they were sitting in that car, why the view even mattered. Half the people said I love you and half the people couldn't say it back.

HISTORY OF OPTIMISM

Like when we got stuck on that deserted island and you said that's it, here's where we live the rest of our lives, we might as well make the best of it, and I said, well, maybe, but maybe, too, we could make a raft by inflating the emptied hearts of these hundreds of lizards running around. And you had already pulled a few palm trees into what looked, from a distance, like a small archway, while I busied myself with the stomping of lizards and the tying off of their tiny and magnificent femoral arteries.

HISTORY OF DEPRESSION SCREENING TESTS

How frequently do you clear or feel like you've cleared a paper jam by following the Clearing A Paper Jam diagram on the inside of an actual or imagined photocopier? How frequently do you pack up and send or feel like you've packed up and sent a package that is elaborately non-rectangular? Ever sipped anything from a metal cup? Angrily disputed points made much earlier in the conversation, possibly years ago, and forgotten now by everyone else, if everyone else was even around back then? Whose rollers and drums wept, and error codes shone the blue of snapped ice?

HISTORY OF LOS ANGELES

Nine out of ten of us are going to die, maybe more. We'll die in houses and hospitals, in cars, on sunny days, under umbrellas, in bed and uncomfortable, in bed and asleep. We'll have conversations before we die, or stay quiet, or write something down, or drift in and out of sleep for sixteen months. We'll have particular shadows cross our thoughts well in advance, or we won't, it'll be pure streaming sunlight until the baby grand crashes down from two floors up. We'll be handed X-rays, we'll be shown MRI video clips, we'll be IV'd and rotated twice a day. We'll say goodbye or not, and remember the wrong things, the things that didn't matter or didn't happen or happened to someone else. We'll sit in wheelchairs, asleep, and falling forward, and the women paid to catch us still catching us.

FOR EVERYTHING TO HAVE HAPPENED

I hate fountains because
they're pointless. Man-made and the
water's recycled.

They're like the Pink Floyd
laser shows in the '90s,
which had no Pink Floyd.

This guy, though, loves them,
so much so he's holding his
iPad up to one.

Meanwhile, yes, of course:
a full moon, several miles of
ocean, and mountains.

And, earlier in
the day, the bee landing on
the bright lavender.

When its wings stopped, the
stem buckled. Our burden is
just a lack of flight.

THE KAFKA FIRST-LINE BLUES

It was summer, a hot day.
It was summer, a hot hot day.
The night was lost, the moon far away.

I have eleven sons.
Oh yes, lord, I have eleven sons.
They see me, lord, and they all run.

It looks as if much had been neglected in our country's system of defense.
Oh, it looks as if much had been neglected in our country's system of defense.
You say you're leaving, but you're not making sense.

We have a new advocate, Dr. Bucephalus.
We have ourselves a new advocate, Dr. Bucephalus.
It was once the whole world, baby, but now it's just us.

FAVORITES

His was landlocked, stop-motion,
the getting and the got. Hers was
how-so and why-some, hers was
clippety clippety clop. His was sleepy
and gone, slunk down, a mudder's track.
Hers was made to keep, and calling now,
and while we're back. His was empty-handed
and three-point turns, his was
a papered head. Hers was stutter step,
and slipshod, and the wretchedly dead.
His was brought in from the outside to,
you know, set things right. Hers was able,
with louvered blinds, to make it night.
His was barely to be. Hers was out to sea.

DEAR CW

Wayward Coffee's stage
was once the worst place one could
be, poetry-wise.

The cash register
ringing, the steamer humming,
and ten open-mic

hopefuls mouthing their
lines. That reading rendered me
illiterate. Now,

though, with Wayward two
miles south and you three time zones
east, it'd be lovely,

seeing you here. Is
it that I missed half of what
made me happy, back

then, and so wasn't?
Or is it that what happens
is always sunk in

deeper misery,
and it's only as memory,
unencumbered by

the weight of what's next,
of what might or might not be,
that meaning is made?

RECASTING OUR SPIRITUAL AMBITION

If "truth" were what I can understand . . . it would end up being but a small truth, my-sized. Truth must reside precisely in what I shall never understand.

—Clarice Lispector

It turns out the my-
sized truth was all we wanted,
after all, and that

anything more was
too much. I'd prefer to know
whether the shelf needs

a bracket every
sixteen inches or every
twenty-four, and not

whether my life has
meaning. Even with brackets,
though, prayer slips in.

Like in *True Romance*,
when Bronson Pinchot dropped to
his knees and begged for

his life: Pinchot was
wearing a wire and talking
not to Christian Slater,

who had a gun to
his head, but Chris Penn, I guess,
if by Chris Penn we

can ever mean some
higher power. Chris Penn/
God only laughed and

Pinchot died an hour
later, though not from Christian
Slater, so, in a

way, his prayer was answered,
albeit in only the
most technical sense.

HYPOTHETICAL MORAL QUANDARY CLERIHEWS

Abraham Lincoln
Avoids death by sinking
Deep into his seat.
The boy behind him leaves in a sheet.

*

Genghis Khan
Is killed earlier on
By time travelers in neoprene suits.
As a kid, say, in a leather crib, and wearing tiny leather boots.

LULLABY

All the rodeo stars
were sleeping in bars
(all the rodeo stars).

All the fishermen's wives
were ending their lives
(all the fishermen's wives).

All the songs for the evening
were songs now of leaving
(all the songs for the evening).

HISTORY OF ANGER

We made a machine for getting angry. We put it on a timer. Every two days, we said. Every week, every year, every hour on the hour. We spot-checked the gears, we dusted the latticework. We changed our mind, we didn't want the machine after all. Too many tubes to care for, too many trips to the machine store, too many days lost to this humming, too many kids gathered around to see what's what, exactly. We put the machine in a box and put the box in the ocean. We put the ocean inside us, wave after wave of it. We held steady.

HISTORY OF DESCRIPTION

You know that old 1950s diner you picture when you think of an Ohio diner? It's not that. You know the shades you think of when someone says denim, western blue jay, the sky above the Grand Canyon? When someone says food coloring? Mold? Not those either. You know that feeling you get when you remember the wrong thing, or the right thing but in the wrong order (you were in Indiana when that happened, the car was a Volvo, the house had two stories, no basement), and as a result the feeling balloons outward, no longer content to just corner your evening? It's not that. You know the replacement for everything they keep offering up now that you're awake, a guest at last in the great hall? It's none of those. Not the toothbrush, not the chair, not the blanket that doesn't reach your feet. You're getting colder.

HISTORY OF TOLD YOU SO

And after it was all over, the dust settled, the graveyard again quiet, the birds migrating once more southward, the trees photosynthesizing in the usual fashion, the rocks made still, the sea back to a blurred surface on which to project any number of dreamlike images, the tractors cutting their standard corners in the field, the beautiful strangers again ignoring the non-beautiful strangers, the horses galloping along the fence, terrified of some small thing, L. shook her head and said, well, didn't I tell you so.

HISTORY OF PLEASURE

Kusama understood that pleasure was an antidote to not having forever to finish, and, in this way, pleasure is always measured. A scoop from a deep steel bowl. Once pleasure is extended, as a net is, to encompass more and more of our outstretched bodies, we should of course feel ill. We should sleep. We should, as Kusama did, work in the day and institutionalize ourselves at night. In this manner, we can explain much of her early work, several thousand of her polka dots, and nearly all of her hills of sculpted penises.

HISTORY OF PARKS

Henry and I went to see you at Carle Park. That's not right, of course; you aren't at Carle Park (you aren't anywhere), but that's how it seemed. A friend had said she'd planted a tree for you, so we walked up to each sapling and wondered if it was yours. Half the trees were green, half were bright yellow. A few were chimeras, yellow and green both, depending on how the sun and the wind had come over them. Near the park's center was a small maple with wood poles supporting it on each side, all yellow leaves, only a foot higher than us. My heart sped up as I approached the plaque, ready to feel sadness sweep over me, the same way you prepare for fear when standing at the edge of a cliff. I am ready to be scared. I am ready to feel. The plaque celebrated the marriage of M. and L., on the occasion of their first anniversary. So not you, then. None of the trees were yours, or you. In the empty shade between trees, you run with Holden, laughing, six years old, cheeks bright red in the wind, your hair tangled, your eyes almost black.

THIS HEAVY LIFTING

The man wanted to be strong, so he lifted trucks, truck stops, small hospitals. Still, he felt that others in his situation would be able to lift more. He lifted golf courses, suburban neighborhoods, the ones with ponds and SUVs. He lifted with one arm the things he could readily lift with two: larger-than-life statues, trains, cosmonaut memorial stadiums. The owners of the lifted items didn't mind so much, this heavy lifting. They asked if they could stay in their cars, or their homes, or swimming in their pools. He always said yes—what else was there to say?—though on occasion some small portion of the lifted people looked unhappy, and he saw that he was not only not supposed to spill their water or keep unshuffled their stone walls, but somehow leave the world both altered and intact, and so felt unhappy himself, and so less strong.

HISTORY OF PEPSI'S CORPORATE STRATEGY

This hat is my backup hat. This spoon is my backup spoon. This coffee is my second coffee. This song is the song I listened to after listening to my favorite song. This wallet is the one I thought I wanted but I didn't want at all. This child is the middle child. This argument is the one that happens after the bigger argument ends, do you know where I put my glasses, just after I don't think we're right for each other. This map is the one we bought when the main map was lost. This plan is plan B. This heart is the Jarvik heart. This hill is down the road from the mountain. This light is fluorescent. This kindness is a while ago.

HISTORY OF HORSE

Horse was bolts and twine and contained no beating heart. Horse was steel hooves, painted plastic tail, saddle soap for the saddle. Horse was clop clop of the fingers on the table. Horse was TV only, movies only, books only, head in the bed only. Horse was flies and rubber cement. Horse was how, when ahead, you could look over your shoulder, the trail behind you a line of dust and sunlight.

CONSIDER THIS NUMBER

Bischoff House was designed by William Etty circa 1725 for the Bischoff family. William Etty, with his tiny, pointed teeth. A fanlight over the front door admits the morning sun. William was one of the smallest fish in the sea at that time (250 million years ago) and adapted to survive in the very salty water. Barley sugar bannister rails, curving to sides of steps. Or, better yet: a landing window with inner wooden shutters. Sharp-toothed Etty loads the bodies of the wagons onto the barges at the canal wharf, which are towed by horses down to Derby. Plaster cornice over the door and sardine-sized William Etty, in July, 1949, nearing hundreds of years old. We designed all of William Etty for tearing flesh, for living in the Zechstein (a warm tropical sea), for telling us as it rains why he is probably not a predator. We are none of us predators, none of us William Ettys.

HISTORY OF ART

He had to admit that he didn't love Alexander Calder's *Eagle* as much as he loved his wife, and that he didn't love his wife as much as he loved his children, and that his children he liked to see fall asleep so he could watch a movie. Once, though, while underneath it, and the blue sky showing through, Calder's *Eagle* seemed to him a terrifying vision of life, caught by orange steel and exposed joints, as though all our junctures could be wrenched loose.

HISTORY OF *THE GRADUATE*, CLOSING SHOT

Take 1. When Hoffman and Ross get on, the bus is empty, except for the driver. The driver stares, shrugs his shoulders, and pulls away from the curb. Cue Simon and Garfunkel.

Take 2. When Hoffman and Ross get on, the bus is filled with third graders in alligator masks, made from real alligators. The kids turn in their seats to watch Hoffman and Ross sit down. Cue Simon and Garfunkel.

Take 3. Same as above, except the kids don't turn in their seats, they just keep looking straight ahead, their eyes pretty grim and unblinking in their lizard-head masks. Cue Simon and Garfunkel.

Take 4. I'm realizing now that the walk to the back of the bus is an ironic retelling of the walk down the aisle. So no alligator masks and the kids can turn in their pews to look at them after all. Cue Simon and Garfunkel.

Take 5. Bob is asking why it's third graders. Might not the tininess of third graders render even the minute Hoffman relatively giant? Bob says there's no practical reason a bus of third graders would even stop to pick up Hoffman and Ross, and plus, isn't it the weekend? The third graders are now not wearing alligator masks and no longer in third grade. Cue Simon and Garfunkel.

Take 6. The woman staring at Hoffman and Ross from two seats up is in her fifties, and heavyset, and wearing lipstick. You should see in her face the potential to have herself done what Hoffman and Ross just did, to have disrupted whatever municipal plans the fates had sketched out for her in their mid-rise office building. You should see in her face, too, that, despite this potential, she never actually did anything of the sort. She has maybe an alligator purse in her lap, but it's not in the shot.

HISTORY OF AQUAMAN

We make Aquaman at a park, in February, after school. Orange shirt, green tights, breathes underwater. By breathes, we mean the vapor given off by a heated object. By underwater, we mean held hard against the grass. By green, we mean black. By shirt, the marker we mark him up with.

We make Aquaman and he comes alive and he asks the same questions he always asks: what's he doing here, what's happened up until right now, why the gray sky all around us. We close his eyes, but carefully this time. We whisper in his ear. We tell him, with all kinds of ceremony, you can breathe underwater. He says (we hear him say) what about up here? What do I do above water? Also breathe, we say.

We make Aquaman following the general instructions for making someone else. We use a compass as a circle. We set the eyes to look the same direction. We have in mind clay angels of the 16th century, but more finned. We have in mind the jar we get to keep him in, the way the plastic wrap goes taut with the rubber band and can be drummed on. By taut, we mean distended. We mean what comes of pressing in without coming apart.

HISTORY OF LYING

We loved you too much and so we stopped loving you. Or I did, I stopped
loving you and said you should be sent off, packed to the furthest reaches and
mailed letters every day or two. We loved you too much and the sky knew and
it was dangerous, the sky knowing. And so we stopped loving you, or I did,
and just in case that didn't work we went inside and closed the door and drew
the curtains and angled the venetian blinds so the ground, not the sun, was
looking through. We loved you too much and the heart would not still and
the day would not end and so we did those things in their place: we stilled,
we ended, we stopped. Or I did. Or I said I did—promised, really, hand over
heart, hope to die.

HISTORY OF DEPRESSION

The sadness is that everything is exactly *this* possible (holding out his hands) and *this* far away (holding out his hands again).

HISTORY OF THE LAND

The Beginning People arrived first. They'd had enough with the old place and wanted somewhere new to spruce up and get ready. Ready for what, asked the Middle People (now here, too, with their arms disappearing into muffs and their warmer pants). For you, for you, always for you. But by this time the Ending People were on their way. They'd been sighted on every horizon, cresting the hill in a crouched run, or rowing in on long sharp-tailed boats, or waiting for the train their transfers clearly were still good for. We'd better change everything we're planning on changing right away, the non-Ending People agreed. But with those disappearing arms and tired legs, what hope did they have? They returned to sweeping and checking the mail and building the small, interior weapons for which they'd become famous, the kind that operate over such short distances you might as well introduce yourselves. Which they did, to no avail, once again. The Ending People were all over them.

NOT THE TREES

The rocks are smooth and red and spilled
across the ground. They work like clouds,
resembling what they're not. The drought
empties the rest of it: all's still

beneath the sun. We stop before
we're halfway there and make a small
half-hearted circle. Is it all
of us who sing? We wanted more,

I guess. More silence, more belief,
more meaning, drawn up from the dead.
We pose for iPhone shots instead,
our faces almost scrubbed of grief.

TRANSLATION

When we say
lullaby,
we mean
don't cry.
Story is
you haven't
heard this yet.
Song is
don't forget.

Previous titles in the Carnegie Mellon Poetry Series

2000

Small Boat with Oars of Different Size, Thom Ward
Post Meridian, Mary Ruefle
Hierarchies of Rue, Roger Sauls
Constant Longing, Dennis Sampson
Mortal Education, Joyce Peseroff
How Things Are, James Richardson
Years Later, Gregory Djanikian
On the Waterbed They Sank to Their Own Levels, Sarah Rosenblatt
Blue Jesus, Jim Daniels
Winter Morning Walks: 100 Postcards to Jim Harrison, Ted Kooser

2001

Day Moon, Jon Anderson
The Origin of Green, T. Alan Broughton
Lovers in the Used World, Gillian Conoley
Quarters, James Harms
Mastodon, 80% Complete, Jonathan Johnson
The Deepest Part of the River, Mekeel McBride
Earthly, Michael McFee
Ten Thousand Good Mornings, James Reiss
The World's Last Night, Margot Schilpp
Sex Lives of the Poor and Obscure, David Schloss
Glacier Wine, Maura Stanton
Voyages in English, Dara Wier

2002

Keeping Time, Suzanne Cleary
Astronaut, Brian Henry
What It Wasn't, Laura Kasischke
Slow Risen Among the Smoke Trees, Elizabeth Kirschner
The Finger Bone, Kevin Prufer
Among the Musk Ox People, Mary Ruefle
The Late World, Arthur Smith

2003
Trouble, Mary Baine Campbell
A Place Made of Starlight, Peter Cooley
Taking Down the Angel, Jeff Friedman
Lives of Water, John Hoppenthaler
Imitation of Life, Allison Joseph
Except for One Obscene Brushstroke, Dzvinia Orlowsky
The Mastery Impulse, Ricardo Pau-Llosa
Casino of the Sun, Jerry Williams

2004
The Women Who Loved Elvis All Their Lives, Fleda Brown
The Chronic Liar Buys a Canary, Elizabeth Edwards
Freeways and Aqueducts, James Harms
Prague Winter, Richard Katrovas
Trains in Winter, Jay Meek
Tristimania, Mary Ruefle
Venus Examines Her Breast, Maureen Seaton
Various Orbits, Thom Ward

2005
Things I Can't Tell You, Michael Dennis Browne
Bent to the Earth, Blas Manuel De Luna
Blindsight, Carol Hamilton
Fallen from a Chariot, Kevin Prufer
Needlegrass, Dennis Sampson
Laws of My Nature, Margot Schilpp
Sleeping Woman, Herbert Scott
Renovation, Jeffrey Thomson

2006
Burn the Field, Amy Beeder
The Sadness of Others, Hayan Charara
A Grammar to Waking, Nancy Eimers
Dog Star Delicatessen: New and Selected Poems 1979–2006, Mekeel McBride
Shinemaster, Michael McFee

In the Land We Imagined Ourselves, Jonathan Johnson
Selected Early Poems: 1958-1983, Greg Kuzma
The Other Life: Selected Poems, Herbert Scott
Admission, Jerry Williams

2011
Having a Little Talk with Capital P Poetry, Jim Daniels
Oz, Nancy Eimers
Working in Flour, Jeff Friedman
Scorpio Rising: Selected Poems, Richard Katrovas
The Politics, Benjamin Paloff
Copperhead, Rachel Richardson

2012
Now Make an Altar, Amy Beeder
Still Some Cake, James Cummins
Comet Scar, James Harms
Early Creatures, Native Gods, K. A. Hays
That Was Oasis, Michael McFee
Blue Rust, Joseph Millar
Spitshine, Anne Marie Rooney
Civil Twilight, Margot Schilpp

2013
Oregon, Henry Carlile
Selvage, Donna Johnson
At the Autopsy of Vaslav Nijinksy, Bridget Lowe
Silvertone, Dzvinia Orlowsky
Fibonacci Batman: New & Selected Poems (1991-2011), Maureen Seaton
When We Were Cherished, Eve Shelnutt
The Fortunate Era, Arthur Smith
Birds of the Air, David Yezzi

2014
Night Bus to the Afterlife, Peter Cooley
Alexandria, Jasmine Bailey